This book belongs to:

_____

_____

_____

To my wonderful parents, Elva and Primitivo: Through your sacrifices, you have always inspired me to be the best I can be. Thank you for believing in me. Los amo. Also, to my husband and two sons, Maxton and Bronx, I love you to the moon and back.

—L.O.

To all my Primas.

— J.C.

immedium

inspiring a world of imagination

Immedium, Inc.
P.O. Box 31846
San Francisco, CA 94131
www.immedium.com

First hardcover edition published 2020

Edited by Don Menn
Book design by Stefanie Liang Chung

Printed in Malaysia
10 9 8 7 6 5 4 3 2 1

Library of Congress Cataloging-in-Publication Data

Names: Ordaz, Leticia, 1976- author. | Calle, Juan, 1977- illustrator.
Title: That girl on TV could be me! : the journey of a Latina news anchor =
    Yo podria ser esa chica en la tele! : el camino de una noticiera latina
    / by Leticia Ordaz ; illustrated by Juan Calle.
Description: San Francisco, CA : Immedium, Inc., [2020] | Audience: Ages
    3-8 | Audience: Grades 2-3 | Summary: "This is an autobiography of a
    Latina TV news anchor. Growing up near Sacramento, CA, little Leticia
    dreams of being a TV newscaster. But no one on TV looks like her. This
    shy, small-town girl overcomes barriers, like her fear of public
    speaking, to become the first in her hardworking Mexican family to
    attend college. Then, starting as an intern, she climbs the ladder,
    travels to different cities, and reports on a rainbow of stories.
    Eventually she lands her dream job: working at her hometown Channel
    3."-- Provided by publisher.
Identifiers: LCCN 2020011254 (print) | LCCN 2020011255 (ebook) | ISBN
    9781597021517 (hardcover) | ISBN 9781597021531 (ebook)
Subjects: LCSH: Ordaz, Leticia, 1976---Juvenile literature. | Television
    news anchors--United States--Biography--Juvenile literature. | CYAC:
    Ordaz, Leticia, 1976- | Television news anchors. | Television
    personalities. | Women--Biography.
Classification: LCC PN1992.4.O69 A3 2020 (print) | LCC PN1992.4.O69
    (ebook) | DDC 070.1/95092--dc23
LC record available at https://lccn.loc.gov/2020011254
LC ebook record available at https://lccn.loc.gov/2020011255

ISBN: 978-1-59702-151-7

That Girl on TV Could Be Me!

¡Yo Podría Ser Esa Chica en la Tele!
El Camino de una Noticiera Latina

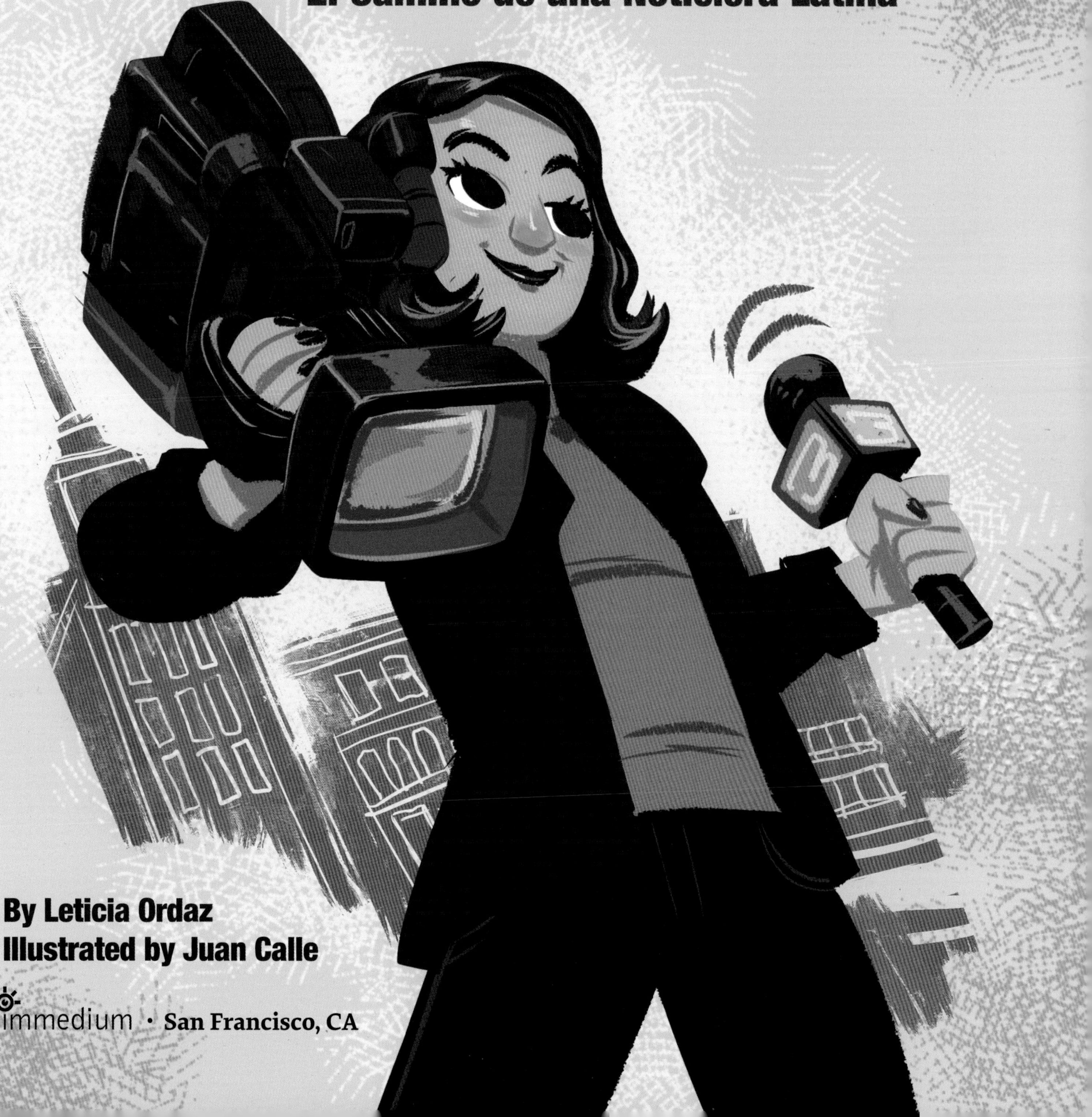

By Leticia Ordaz

Illustrated by Juan Calle

immedium · San Francisco, CA

In the small California town of Galt, a five-year-old Latina watched the news. Her Mami said: "Lety, turn the TV off. It's dinnertime."

I was that girl. I asked my Mami, "Why doesn't anyone look like me on TV?"

En la pequeña ciudad de Galt, California, una Latina de cinco años veía las noticias. Mami dijo: "Lety, apaga la tele. Es hora de cenar."

Yo era esa niña. Le pregunté a Mami: "¿Por qué nadie se parece a mí en la tele?"

Mami replied, "Don't worry. One day, after you go to college, you could be on the news, too."

She and Papi inspired me to work hard to achieve my dreams, just like they had theirs.

Mami respondió: "No te preocupes. Un día, después de ir a la universidad, tú también podrías estar en las noticias."

Ella y Papi me inspiraron a trabajar duro para alcanzar mis sueños, tal como lo hicieron ellos.

I wanted to be on TV, but I was the shy girl in class. When my sixth-grade teacher, Mr. Heinrich, called on me to read aloud, I was nervous. I spoke so quietly that my classmates shouted, "Speak up, Leticia!"

Yo quería estar en la tele, pero era la niña tímida en clase. Cuando mi maestro de sexto grado, Sr. Heinrich, pidió que leyera en voz alta, estaba nerviosa. Hablé tan bajito que mis compañeros gritaron: "¡Habla alto, Leticia!"

When I got home, I locked myself in my room.
I practiced reading in front of the mirror for two hours.

"You can do this," I thought. "The next time the teacher calls my name, I will read loud and proud."

Cuando llegué a casa, me encerré en mi cuarto.
Practiqué leyendo frente al espejo por dos horas.
"Puedes hacer esto," pensé. "La próxima vez que el maestro diga mi nombre, leeré fuerte y con orgullo."

My parents encouraged me to do well in school. In Michoacán, Mexico, they left school after the sixth grade to support their families. They immigrated to the United States to give me and my sister Lorena a better life.

Mis padres me animaron a salir bien en la escuela. En Michoacán, México, ellos dejaron la escuela después de sexto grado para ayudar a mantener a sus familias. Ellos inmigraron a los Estados Unidos para darnos a mí y a mi hermana

If only I had perfect teeth, I'd have a confident smile. In high school, I begged my parents for braces. Papi picked grapes and got a new job. My parents used their savings to reward me for getting good grades.

Si tan solo tuviera mis dientes perfectos, tendría una sonrisa segura. En la escuela secundaria, le rogué a mis padres para usar frenos. Papi piscó uvas y consiguió un trabajo nuevo. Mis padres usaron sus ahorros para recompensarme por obtener buenas calificaciones.

I entered the Galt pageant Señorita Independencia de Mexico to celebrate my Latina culture. I wasn't a good dancer and didn't win. But I made friends and was awarded Miss Photogenic and a college scholarship.

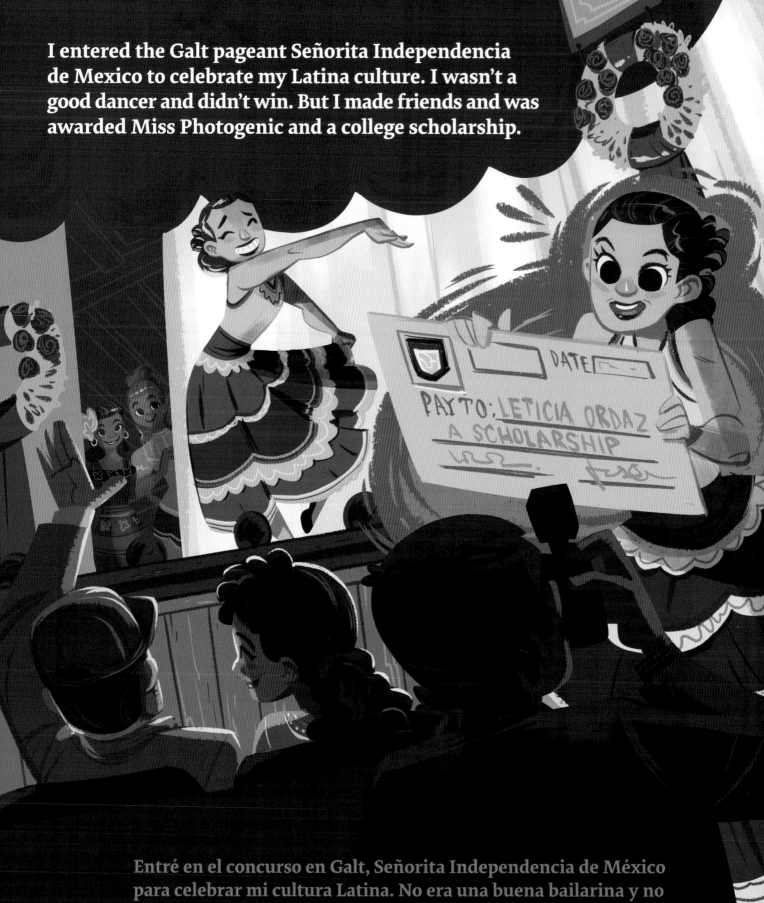

Entré en el concurso en Galt, Señorita Independencia de México para celebrar mi cultura Latina. No era una buena bailarina y no gané. Pero hice amistades y gané el premio Miss Fotogénica y una beca universitaria.

After Lorena graduated Galt High, she went to work. But I wanted to attend college to show my cousins and little brother Javier another path. I enrolled at Sacramento State, a beautiful campus full of trees.

LORENA EN EL TRABAJO ♡

MI HERMANITO JAVIER ☺

Después que Lorena se graduó de Galt High, se fue a trabajar. Pero yo quería ir a la universidad para demostrarle a mis primos y mi hermanito Javier otro camino. Me inscribí en Sacramento State, una hermosa universidad llena de árboles.

I started studying theater but switched to Communications. Students ran their own newscast on cable access TV, so I wanted to learn and practice as much as possible. We wrote and shot our reports, and I was an anchor.

I applied for an internship at my dream television station: Channel 3 in Sacramento. I got accepted! I was so excited that I baked brownies to make friends there and tag along with news crews.

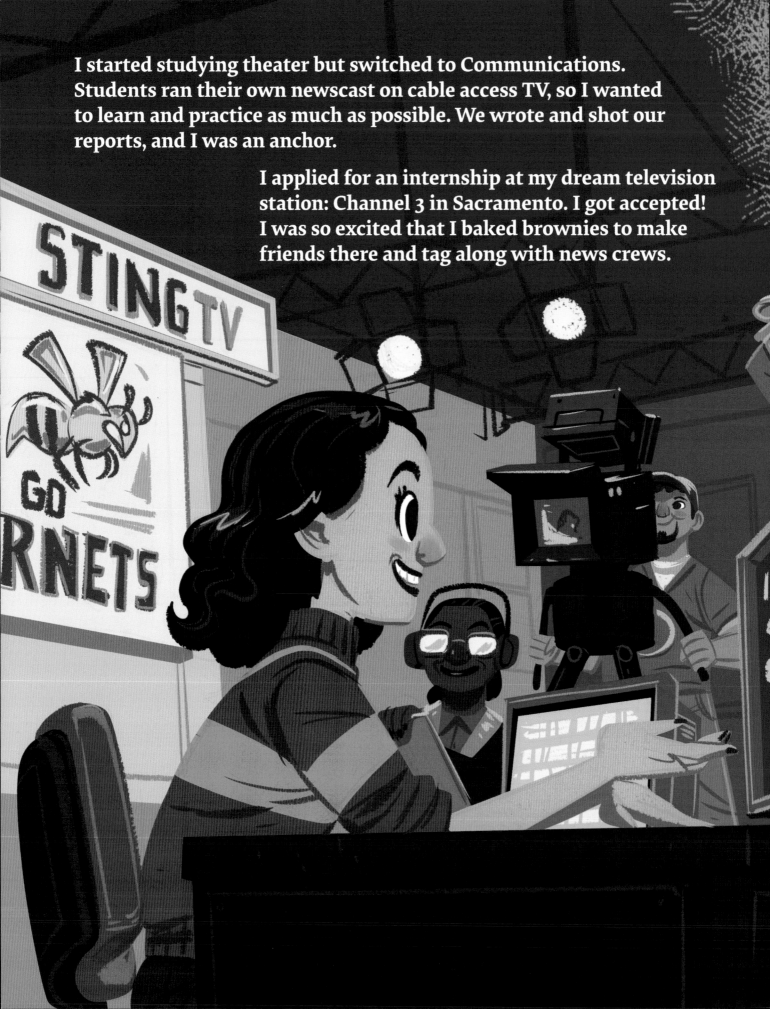

Empecé estudiando teatro, pero cambié a Comunicaciones. Los estudiantes tenían su propio noticiario en la televisión de acceso por cable, así que quería aprender y practicar tanto como pudiera. Escribíamos y grabábamos nuestros reportajes y yo era presentadora de noticias.

Apliqué a un internado en la estación de televisión de mis sueños: el Canal 3 en Sacramento. ¡Me aceptaron! Estaba tan emocionada que horneé brownies para hacer amigos allí y acompañar a los equipos de noticieros.

veterans took me under their wings. Producer Steve Mellish advised: "Don't ever tell someone you want to be an anchor. You must work for that title."

Los veteranos me guiaron. El productor Steve Mellish me aconsejó: "Nunca le digas a alguien que quieres ser presentadora de noticias. Debes de trabajar para ese título."

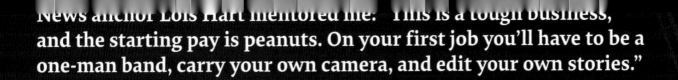

News anchor Lois Hart mentored me: "This is a tough business, and the starting pay is peanuts. On your first job you'll have to be a one-man band, carry your own camera, and edit your own stories."

Lois Hart, presentadora de noticias, me comentó: "Este es un negocio difícil y el sueldo inicial es apenas nada. En tú primer trabajo tendrás que hacer todo tú sola, llevar tu propia cámara y editar tus propios reportajes."

Unafraid, I accompanied reporters to snowstorms! In a satellite truck, we dropped off photographer Rob Stewart to shoot video. When we found him later, he was practically frozen!

Sin miedo, ¡acompañé a reporteros a la nieve! En un camión satelital, dejamos al fotógrafo Rob Stewart para grabar video. Cuando lo encontramos más tarde, ¡estaba prácticamente congelado!

Photographers patiently helped me practice "stand-ups" on roadsides and in rainstorms. Sometimes I needed twenty takes to get it right! I wanted to be a reporter and mailed my video résumés to two hundred TV stations.

Los fotógrafos me ayudaron pacientemente a practicar "frente a cámara" en los lados de la carretera y en aguaceros. ¡A veces necesitaba 20 tomas para hacerlo bien! Quería ser reportera y envié mis vídeos de résumés por correo a 200 estaciones de televisión.

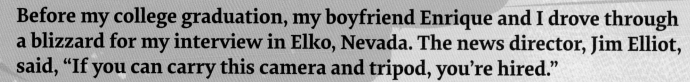

Before my college graduation, my boyfriend Enrique and I drove through a blizzard for my interview in Elko, Nevada. The news director, Jim Elliot, said, "If you can carry this camera and tripod, you're hired."

Antes de mi graduación universitaria, mi novio Enrique y yo manejamos con una tormenta de nieve para llegar a mi entrevista de trabajo en Elko, Nevada.

El director de noticias, Jim Elliot, dijo: "Si puedes cargar esta cámara y el

The equipment weighed 65 pounds. I was 95 pounds. Still, I answered, "Yes, I can." I began my dream career making minimum wage at $8 an hour. Just like my parents, I had to leave my hometown to achieve my goals.

El equipo pesaba 65 libras y yo 95 libras pero respondí: "Sí, puedo." Comencé la carrera de mis sueños ganando el salario mínimo de $8 la hora. Al igual que mis padres, tuve que dejar mi pueblo para lograr mis metas.

Before Christmas, I became the first in my family to graduate from college. As I put on my cap and gown, tears of joy rolled down my proud parents' faces. They sacrificed to give us the opportunity to do more with our lives.

Antes de Navidad, me convertí en la primera en mi familia en graduarse de la universidad. Al ponerme la gorra y bata, las lágrimas de alegría rodaron por los rostros de mis padres orgullosos. Ellos se sacrificaron para darnos la oportunidad de hacer lo mejor con nuestras vidas.

On New Year's Day, I left for Elko. My parents drove me in a moving truck with my bed and belongings over the snowy Sierras. At the small TV station, I met the morning anchor Ellen Chang.

El día de Año Nuevo, me marché a Elko. Mis padres me llevaron en un camión de mudanza con mi cama y pertenencias sobre la Sierra Nevada. En la pequeña estación de televisión, conocí a la presentadora de las noticias de la mañana Ellen Chang.

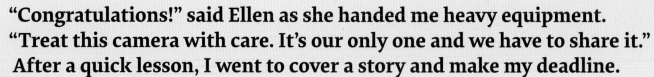

"Congratulations!" said Ellen as she handed me heavy equipment. "Treat this camera with care. It's our only one and we have to share it." After a quick lesson, I went to cover a story and make my deadline.

"¡Felicidades!" dijo Ellen mientras me entregaba el equipo pesado. "Trata esta cámara con cuidado. Es la única que tenemos y hay que compartirla." Después de una lección rápida, fui a cubrir un reportaje con tiempo límite.

I covered Cowboy Poetry Day. Western wranglers shared stories and songs before an admiring audience. My first stand-up was blurry and a bust. But I told myself: "I will get this right!"

Cubrí el Día de la Poesía Vaquera. Los vaqueros compartieron historias y canciones ante un público admirador. Mi primer "frente a cámara" fue borroso y un fracaso. Pero me dije: ";Lo haré bien!"

For more than a year, I wrote my own stories, shot video, prepared on-air interviews, did my own make-up, and edited reports. However, I was homesick for California, my family, and my Mami's flour tortillas.

Por más de un año, escribí mis propias historias, grabé video, preparé entrevistas al aire, me maquillaje yo misma y edité reportajes. Sin embargo, extrañaba a California, mi familia y las tortillas de harina de mi Mami.

Just then, I got a call from Bakersfield.
KGET news director Jack Bowe proposed:
"I can offer you a job, plus a cameraman to
go with you on stories." That was my lucky
day and I accepted!

En ese momento, recibí una llamada de
Bakersfield. El director de noticias de KGET
Jack Bowe dijo: "Puedo ofrecerte un trabajo
y también un camarógrafo que te acompañe
a tus reportajes." ¡Ese fue mi día de suerte y
acepté la propuesta!

My first story and live shot was covering a bear... in my apartment complex. I remembered meteorologist Rob Mayeda's advice: "If you don't have a script, keep it short, simple and to the point, and describe what you are seeing."

Mi primera historia y reporte en vivo fue cubriendo a un oso... en mi complejo de apartamentos. Recordé el consejo del meteorólogo Rob Mayeda: "Si no tienes un guión, mantenlo corto, simple y al grano y describe lo que estás viendo."

Next, I worked for the Fox station in Fresno.
Once, I was wrapped up by a snake at the county fair.

Covering honeybees at an almond orchard,
my photographer and I were bitten by a
scourge of mosquitoes.

Luego, trabajé para la estación de
Fox en Fresno. Una vez, fui envuelta
por una serpiente en la feria del

Reportando sobre abejas en un
huerto de almendras, mi fotógrafo
y yo fuimos picados por una nube

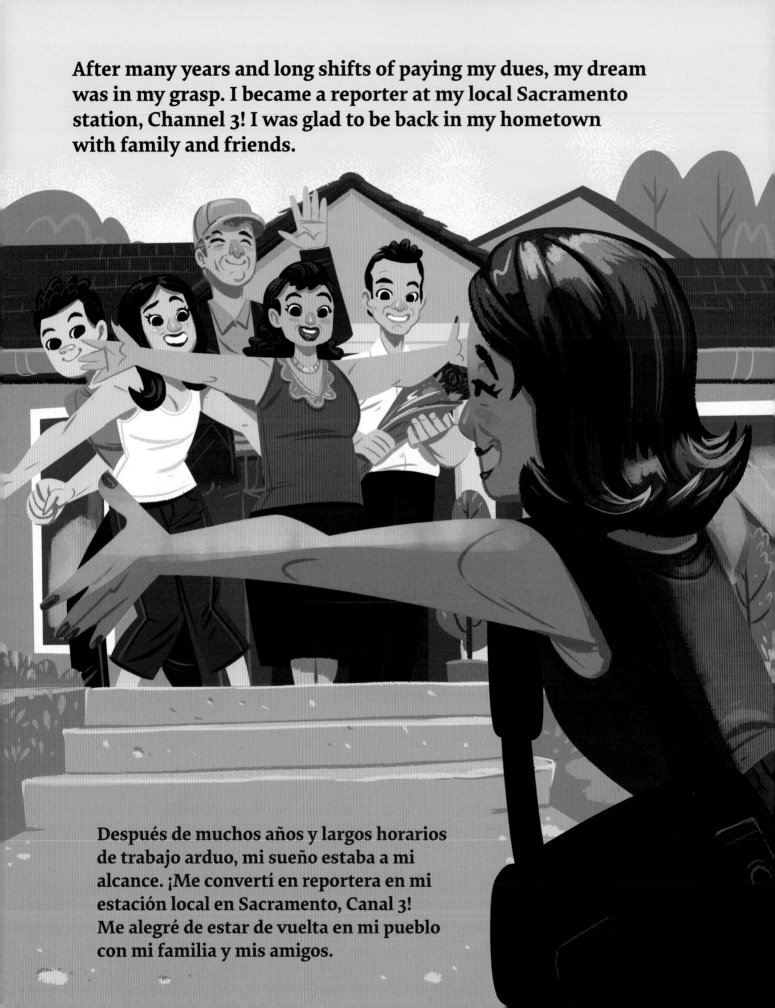

After many years and long shifts of paying my dues, my dream was in my grasp. I became a reporter at my local Sacramento station, Channel 3! I was glad to be back in my hometown with family and friends.

Después de muchos años y largos horarios de trabajo arduo, mi sueño estaba a mi alcance. ¡Me convertí en reportera en mi estación local en Sacramento, Canal 3! Me alegré de estar de vuelta en mi pueblo con mi familia y mis amigos.

My most memorable stories involved animals and helping people. At a dairy farm, Big Lucy the cow splashed me with poop.

Then, at a surfing park, a giant wave wiped me out on live TV.

Mis reportajes más memorables involucraron animales y ayudar a la gente. En una granja lechera, la vaca Big Lucy me salpicó de popó.

Luego, en un parque de surf, una ola gigante me tumbó en vivo.

Happily, I married Enrique. After my seven years in the broadcast business, Enrique and I started a family. But now that I was pregnant, I worried, "Maybe some viewers won't want to see me on TV anymore."

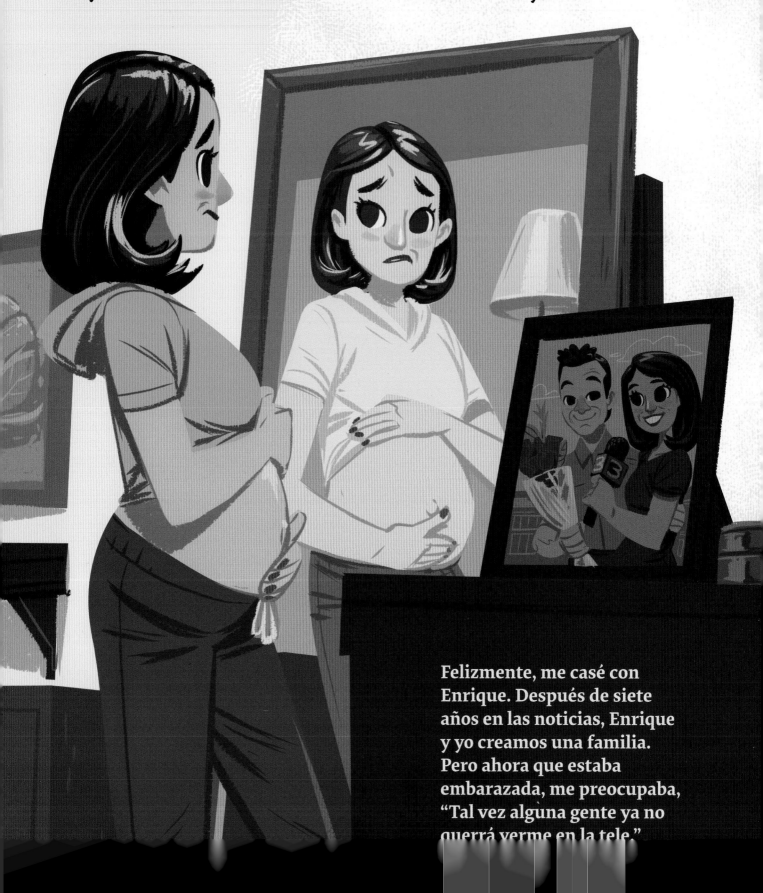

Felizmente, me casé con Enrique. Después de siete años en las noticias, Enrique y yo creamos una familia. Pero ahora que estaba embarazada, me preocupaba, "Tal vez alguna gente ya no querrá verme en la tele."

I was wrong. My newsroom boss, Lori Waldon, surprised me by announcing, "You will now be an anchor."

I was relieved and overjoyed that I could grow my family and career at the same time.

Me equivoqué. Mi jefa de noticias, Lori Waldon, me sorprendió al anunciar: "Ahora serás presentadora." Me sentí aliviada y muy contenta de poder tener mi familia y desarrollar mi carrera al mismo tiempo.

Now we have two little boys. Maxton and Bronx see their mommy on the news and melt my heart every time they tell me: "Mami, we're proud of you for reading to the whole city."

Ahora tenemos dos niños pequeños. Maxton y Bronx ven a su mami en las noticias y mi corazón se derrite cada vez que me dicen: "Mami, estamos orgullosos de ti por leerle a toda la ciudad."

In 2018, for breaking news, I rushed to Butte County to cover the Camp Fire. It was the most destructive fire in California's history. I hugged families who lost their homes, but not their hope.

En 2018, para noticias de última hora, me apresuré al condado de Butte para cubrir el incendio de Camp. Fue el incendio más destructivo en la historia de California. Abracé a las familias que perdieron sus hogares, pero no su esperanza.

Through it all, I love talking about my job with students. Sometimes I have them practice speaking with a microphone. My biggest reward is helping the shy ones.

Después de todo, me encanta hablar de mi carrera con estudiantes. A veces los dejo practicar hablando en un micrófono. Mi mayor recompensa es ayudar a los tímidos.

I tell them: "Dreams can come true... no matter the color of your skin or where you come from. You will face hardships. But you have to believe in yourself."

Les digo: "Los sueños pueden hacerse realidad... no importa el color de tu piel o de dónde vengas. Enfrentarás dificultades. Pero tienes que creer en ti mismo."

GLOSSARY

Access Cable TV
Acceso a TV por cable
A non-commercial station where the public can create programs.

Anchor
Presentadora de Noticias
The newscaster in the studio who addresses the audience at home or online.

Breaking News
Noticias de última hora
Reports on recent events that lead the newscast or interrupt regularly scheduled programs.

Broadcast Journalism
Periodismo audiovisual
News transmitted to a large audience by radio, television, or online.

Camera
Cámara
Portable equipment that records video and audio (with a microphone).

Crew
Equipo
A reporter and photographer, and sometimes a field producer and audio person.

Deadline
Tiempo limite
The time when a reporter must deliver a story to a producer, editor, or photographer to make air.

Director
Director/a
Supervisor of the newscast's components which the audience sees.

Editor
Editor/a
Person who cuts, mixes, and finalizes the audio and video that are shown on a newscast.

Live shot
Reporte en Vivo
When a TV reporter provides a news report (that isn't pre-recorded) at a remote location.

Make-up
Maquillaje
Facial cosmetics (ex. lipstick) applied to enhance one's broadcast appearance.

Meteorlogist
Meteorólogo/a
Weatherperson who forecasts local climate and atmospheric conditions.

Microphone
Micrófono
Electronic equipment that records audio (speech or sound).

News
Noticias
Information that is new, interesting, or important.

Newscast
Noticiero
A news program broadcast on television or radio.

Newsroom
Sala de Noticias
The office where journalists are assigned stories, work, and produce news content.

On-air
Al aire
Being broadcast on television or radio to an audience.

Photographer
Fotógrafo/a
Person who operates the camera to record news stories (with a reporter) to present on-air.

Producer
Productor/a
Person who plans, writes, and selects the arrangement of stories on the TV newscast.

Reporter
Reportero/a
A journalist who researches, interviews, writes news, and then presents stories on camera.

Résumé
Résumé
Summary of qualifications (often paired with examples) used to apply for a job.

Satellite Truck
Camión satelital
Truck that transmits news on location by satellite to the station.

Script
Guión
The text of a news report written by a journalist (such as a producer, reporter, or anchor).

Shift
Horario
A period of time for working during the day, evening, or night.

Shot
Toma de cámara
One scene recorded by camera, uninterrupted by editing, interruptions, or cuts.

Stand up
Frente a cámara
A correspondent reports on camera with a short commentary from a recorded news segment.

Station
Estación
A facility (building or headquarters) that broadcasts television or radio programs.

Take
Toma
One attempt by a reporter and photographer to make a successful shot with a particular camera setup.

Tripod
Trípode
A three-legged portable stand for a camera.

Video
Video
The visual portion of a TV broadcast; short for videotape.

*2019 RTDNA/Hofstra University Newsroom Survey